·ᴛʜᴇPLEASANCE·

A Pleasance Theatre Trust,
Up In Arms
and Ellie Keel
co-production

In Lipstick

by Annie Jenkins

T0333383

First performed at the Pleasance Theatre,
Islington, London
8–27 January 2019.

Pleasance Islington
Carpenters Mews
North Rd
London N7 9EF

www.pleasance.co.uk

In Lipstick

by Annie Jenkins

Maud	**Caroline Faber**
Cynthia	**Alice Sykes**
Dennis	**James Doherty**

Director	**Alice Hamilton**
Designer	**Delyth Evans**
Lighting Designer	**Simon Gethin Thomas**
Sound Designer	**Ed Clarke**
Production Manager	**Jack Greenyer**
Stage Manager	**Lucy Morris**
Producer	**Ellie Keel**
Producer	**Barney Norris** (for Up In Arms)
Producer	**Nic Connaughton** (for Pleasance Theatre)

Cast

Caroline Faber | Maud

Theatre credits include: *Network* and *The Heiress* (National Theatre);
My Mother Said I Never Should (St James Theatre); *Romeo and Juliet*
and *Paradise Lost* (Headlong Theatre); *The Terrors of the Night* (Sam
Wanamaker Playhouse); *King Lear* (Young Vic); *Hangover Square*
(Finborough Theatre); *Keepers of the Flame* (RSC/Live Theatre) *The
Taming of the Shrew, Edward III, The Malcontent, Here Lies Mary Spindler*
(RSC); *Piaf* (Bolton, Octagon); *The Norman Conquests, Last Easter* (Birm-
ingham Rep); *Dangerous Corner* (Garrick Theatre); *Tender* (Hampstead
Theatre); *Mill on the Floss* (Shared Experience); *The Colonel Bird* (The
Gate, Notting Hill); *Top Girls* (Theatre Royal Plymouth); *Kanye the First*
(HighTide); *The End of the Affair, Vermillion Dream* and *The Merchant of
Venice* (Salisbury Playhouse); *Cavalcade* (Sadlers Wells). Television credits
include: *Berlin Station, Merlin, Midsomer Murders, Foyle's War, A Good
Murder, My Spy Family, Casualty, Holby City, The Bill, Gamesmaster.*

Alice Sykes | Cynthia

Theatre credits include *A Small Family Business* (National Theatre);
Responsible Other (Hampstead Theatre); *Polar Bears* (Donmar Warehouse,
directed by Jamie Lloyd). Television credits include: *Criminal Justice, Vera,
Midsomer Murders, Silent Witness, Cradle to the Grave, Flea*. Film credits
include: *After Louise.*

James Doherty | Dennis

Theatre credits include: *Fatherland* (Lyric Hammersmith); *London Road,
NT:50, Beyond Caring* (National Theatre); *Aladdin* (Lyric, Hammersmith);
Eventide (Arcola); *Chicago* (Garrick); *Marguerite* (Theatre Royal
Haymarket); *Les Miserables* (Palace Theatre); *Kiss Me Kate* (Royal Albert
Hall); *God of Carnage* (Northampton Theatre Royal); *Teenage Kicks*
(Edinburgh Festival); *Teechers* (Haymarket); *House and Garden*
(Harrogate Theatre); *Gangster No 1, Harlequinade* and *Separate Tables*
(King's Head). Television credits include: *Queens of Mystery, Clique, Call
the Midwife, The Windsors, Veep, The Thick of It, Him and The Wedding,
Rev, Miranda, The IT Crowd, Delicious, From the Cradle to the Grave, The
Job Lot, Phoneshop, Count Arthur Strong, A Touch of Cloth, Top Coppers,
Boomers, Mongrels, Katy Brand Show, Todd Margaret, Watson and Oliver,
Give Out Girls, Rides, The Royal Bodyguard, Small Potatoes, Endeavour,
Ambassadors, Suspicion, Londoners, The Jury, The Royal, Peak Practice,
Footballers Wives, Night and Day, Is Harry on the Boat, EastEnders,
Coronation Street, Waterloo Road, Casualty, Holby City, Doctors, The Bill,
2.4 Children, In Sickness and in Health, Dad, Hippies, Hotel Getaway, Bob
Martin, The Wyvern Mystery, The Slightly Filthy Show, According to Bex,
All About George*. Film credits include: *London Road, In the Loop, Kat and
the Band, MSND, The Forgotten, Inbred, Closed Circuit, Deviation, Verity's
Summer, City Rats, Backbeat.*

Creatives and Production

Annie Jenkins | Writer

Annie has written two full-length plays, *Staying At Stacey's* and *In Lipstick*. In 2016 her first play, *In Lipstick*, received two rehearsed readings, one as part of the Arcola's new writing festival PlayWROUGHT, and another as part of Druid Theatre's *Druid Debuts* season for the Galway International Arts Festival. It was also shortlisted for the Theatre 503 playwriting award and is receiving its first full performance at The Pleasance, Islington, in January 2019. Annie has also written and co-directed *Funemployed*, a short film about a masochistic, unemployed graduate who develops an obsessive crush on David Cameron. *Funemployed* was screened as part of the 2017 London Short Film Festival, Encounters Film Festival and Underwire Film Festival. It won Shooting People's Film of the Month, March 2017, judged by Anna Biller. In 2014, as part of Shakespeare in Shoreditch, Annie wrote 1000 micro plays over the course of the festival's ten-day duration. In April 2016 all 1000 plays (known as *Annie's 1000 Plays*) were performed at various locations across Hackney. Other work includes: *Lunch in My Car* and *Brave New Word* (Theatre N16); *Sing a Song of Silence* (Arcola Youth Theatre); *What about England?* (Slingshot at Salford's Islington Mill and also published at Orlando online); *50% Lesbian, 100% Scared* (Park Scratchings at the Park Theatre, Made in LDN Bridge at Bunker Theatre); *Tinder471* (90s Season at STYX/pluck.presents at the Old Red Lion); *My Son is in the Kitchen Eating a Biscuit (*HighTide Festival Walthamstow). In 2017 Annie took part in the HighTide Writers' Group and was shortlisted for the Old Vic 12. She graduated with a First in Drama from the University of Manchester in 2013, and is from North London.

Alice Hamilton | Director

Alice is a theatre director, dramaturg, and co-artistic director of Up In Arms theatre company. Having founded Up In Arms with the writer Barney Norris while still a student, she has developed the organisation into an acclaimed touring theatre producer, recognised as 'a company whose practice is exemplary' (Paul Miller, Artistic Director, Orange Tree Theatre) that has 'introduced a new appetite for theatrical quietism' (Michael Billington, *Theatre Record*) into the contemporary cultural landscape. Her productions for Up In Arms include: David Storey's *The March On Russia* (***** Telegraph); Robert Holman's *German Skerries* (**** Guardian, Evening Standard, Whatsonstage); Barney Norris's *Visitors* (***** Times, Financial Times, Evening Standard, Stage, Whatsonstage); *Eventide* (**** Guardian, Times, Evening Standard) and *While We're Here* (**** Times, Financial Times, Time Out). Other theatre includes: Richard Molloy's *Every Day I Make Greatness Happen* (Hampstead Theatre); Barney Norris's *Echo's End* (Salisbury Playhouse); Johnny Donahoe's *Thirty Christmases* (Supporting Wall); Judith Burnley's *Anything That Flies* (Jermyn Street

Theatre); Matt Grinter's *Orca* and Austin Pendleton's *Orson's Shadow* (Southwark Playhouse). She has been a staff director at the National Theatre and has led development and dramaturgical projects at the Royal Court, the National Theatre, Salisbury Playhouse and HighTide.

Delyth Evans | Designer

Delyth recently graduated from the Royal Welsh College of Music and Drama, with a first class in Design For Performance. She now works as both a designer and assistant in London and Wales. Her recent credits include: *Out of Love* (LAMDA); *All That* (Kings Head Theatre); *Rhybudd: Iaith Anweddus* (National Eisteddfod of Wales 2018) and *Punk Rock* (RWCMD).

Simon Gethin Thomas | Lighting Designer

Simon trained for a Master's Degree at the Royal Welsh College of Music and Drama. Lighting Design credits for Up In Arms include: *German Skerries* (Orange Tree Theatre); *Eventide* (Arcola Theatre); *Visitors* (Bush Theatre) and *Fear of Music* (UK tours). Other credits include: *Battleface, The Rest of Your Life* and *One Cold Dark Night* (Bush Theatre: 'This Place We Know'); *The Turn of the Screw* (Clapham Omnibus); *Mrs Orwell* (Southwark Playhouse); *Pincher Martin* (Royal College of Music); *The Blue Bird* (Theatre503); *Stone Face* (Finborough Theatre) and *Sea Fret* (HighTide Festival / Old Red Lion).

Ed Clarke | Sound Designer

Ed is a sound designer and composer based in Otley, UK. Recent designs include: *When We Were Brothers* (Freedom Studios); *Leave Taking* (Bush Theatre); *A Christmas Carol* and *A Short History of Tractors in Ukrainian* (Hull Truck); Middle Child's *All We Ever Wanted . . .* (Hull, Edinburgh, Latitude); *A Super Happy Story* (*About Feeling Super Sad*); *Shirley Valentine* (UK tour); *The Royale* (Bush Theatre); Improbable Theatre's *Beauty and the Beast* (Young Vic, UK tour, Abron's New York, Chicago Museum of Contemporary Art); *Frankenstein* (National Theatre); *Baddies* (Unicorn Theatre); *Show Boat* (New London Theatre); *Nine Lives* (Leeds Studio and touring); *Orpheus* (Battersea Arts Centre, UK tour, Salzburg Festival); *Backbeat* (Duke of York's Theatre); *The Wiz* (Birmingham Rep and West Yorkshire Playhouse); *His Teeth* (Only Connect) and *The Railway Children* (Waterloo International Station and Toronto).

Jack Greenyer | Production Manager

Jack recently completed his final year of the Royal Central School of Speech and Drama's BA Theatre Practice: Technical and Production Management course. He has since been working with theatre companies such as Complicite, National Youth Theatre, Yard Theatre, Soho Theatre and Big House Theatre Company. Jack continues to help creative practitioners make the most of their spaces through his work with his company, Infinity Technical and Production Services

Ellie Keel | Producer

Ellie became an independent theatre producer after working for two years with Thelma Holt, the Oxford Playhouse and the Cameron Mackintosh Foundation. She now produces new plays both independently and on behalf of organisations including The North Wall, The Big House, Heretic Productions, and Forward Arena. For The North Wall she co-founded and produces the annual Alchymy Festival of new plays. With Heretic Productions she co-founded and produces 'Heretic Voices', a national competition and festival of new plays in monologue form. Her work in London includes Hal Coase's *Callisto: a Queer Epic*, which transferred to Arcola Theatre from the Edinburgh Fringe, *Home Chat* by Noël Coward at the Finborough Theatre, Virginia Woolf's *Mrs Dalloway* adapted by Hal Coase at Arcola Theatre, and *Loose Lips* by Katherine Soper at Stoke Newington Town Hall. She trained with Stage One. Ellie is a Director of LGBT+ youth charity Just Like Us and a Trustee of the King's Hall Trust for the Arts

UP IN ARMS

Up In Arms is a multi-award-winning touring theatre company
from the south west of England.

We tell stories about people and the places they're from.

We have presented work in theatres, woods and village halls across the UK,
in co-production or in association with Pleasance Theatre, Arcola Theatre,
Bush Theatre, Orange Tree Theatre, Out of Joint Theatre Company, The
North Wall Arts Centre and Reading Rep. We are an associate company
of Nuffield Southampton Theatres, Farnham Maltings,
Watford Palace Theatre and The North Wall.

Our projects draw on a wide range of artists and collaborators,
but always begin with the ideas of three people:

Alice Hamilton | Co-Artistic Director

Direction for Up In Arms includes: *The March On Russia* (Orange Tree);
While We're Here (Bush Theatre, Farnham Maltings and tour);
German Skerries (Orange Tree and tour); *Eventide* (Arcola and tour);
Visitors (Arcola, Bush Theatre and tour); *Fear of Music* (tour with Out of
Joint) and *At First Sight* (tour and Latitude Festival). Other theatre
includes: *Paradise* and *Every Day I Make Greatness Happen* (Hampstead
Theatre); *Echo's End* (Salisbury Playhouse); *Thirty Christmases*
(Supporting Wall); *Orca* (Papatango at Southwark Playhouse)
and *Orson's Shadow* (Southwark Playhouse).

Barney Norris | Co-Artistic Director

Barney's plays include *Nightfall*, *While We're Here*, *Echo's End*, *Eventide*
and *Visitors* (winner of the Critics' Circle Award for Most Promising
Playwright). He has published two novels, *Turning For Home* and *Five
Rivers Met on a Wooded Plain*, which was a *Times* bestseller
and won a Betty Trask Award, and two non-fiction studies, *To Bodies
Gone: the Theatre of Peter Gill* and *The Wellspring: Conversations with
David Owen Norris*. He is the Martin Esslin Playwright in Residence at
Keble College, Oxford, and has been named by the Evening Standard
as one of the 1000 Most Influential Londoners.

Charlie Young | Company Stage Manager

Charlie has worked around the UK and across the world at venues
including Sydney Opera House, the Lyric, the Vaudeville, the Barbican
the Arts Theatre as a stage manager for Kenny Wax, Nick Brooke Ltd,
Tall Stories, Mischief Theatre, The Wrong Crowd, House, Arcola,
Southwark Playhouse, The Point in Eastleigh, Trafalgar Studios and
many others. For Up In Arms she has stage managed *Fear of Music*,
Visitors, *Eventide*, *German Skerries*, *While We're Here*
and *The March On Russia*.

·PLEASANCE·

Pleasance Theatre Trust

Pleasance Edinburgh opened as part of the 1985 Festival Fringe with two theatres facing onto a deserted courtyard-cum-car-park at an unfashionable eastern end of Edinburgh's Old Town.

Thirty seasons later the Pleasance has become one of the biggest and most highly respected venues at the Edinburgh Festival Fringe, with an international profile and a network of alumni that reads like a who's who of contemporary comedy, drama and entertainment.

Pleasance Islington has been one of the most exciting Off-West-End theatres in London since it opened its doors in 1995, providing a launch pad for some of the most memorable productions and renowned practitioners of the past decade and staying true to its mission of providing a platform for the talent of the future. Across three-spaces, the theatre welcomes artists at all stages of their careers, with a commitment to new work that pushes boundaries.

Pleasance Islington plays host to some of the biggest names in comedy and the likes of Michael McIntyre, Russell Brand, Micky Flanagan, Mark Watson, Adam Hills and Mark Thomas have all regularly complemented our comedy programme.

In Lipstick

Annie Jenkins has written two full-length plays, *In Lipstick* and *Staying at Stacey's*. In 2016 *In Lipstick* had two rehearsed readings: as part of 'PlayWROUGHT' at the Arcola and of Druid Theatre's 'Druid Debuts' season for the Galway International Arts Festival. It was also shortlisted for the Theatre503 Award. In 2018 she wrote *Turned My Head* as part of *VOID* at VAULT Festival, winning a VAULT Innovation Award as well as writing and producing *A Tinder Trilogy* at the Hen and Chickens Theatre as part of the Camden Fringe. She wrote and co-directed *Funemployed*, which was screened at various festivals including the London Short Film Festival in 2017. Short plays include: *Sing a Song of Silence* (Arcola Youth Theatre), *What About England?* (Islington Mill), *Lunch in My Car* (Theatre N16), *50% Lesbian, 100% Scared* (Park Theatre/Bunker Theatre) and *Annie's 1000 Plays* (Shakespeare in Shoreditch). She took part in the first HighTide Writers' Group.

ANNIE JENKINS

In Lipstick

ff

FABER & FABER

First published in 2019
by Faber and Faber Limited
74–77 Great Russell Street
London WC1B 3DA

Typeset by Country Setting, Kingsdown, Kent CT14 8ES
Printed in England by CPI Group (UK) Ltd, Croydon CR0 4YY

© Annie Jenkins, 2019

Annie Jenkins is hereby identified as author
of this work in accordance with Section 77
of the Copyright, Designs and Patents Act 1988

A CIP record for this book is available from the British Library

ISBN 978-0-571-35456-6

2 4 6 8 10 9 7 5 3 1

In Lipstick, produced by the Up In Arms company, was first performed at the Pleasance, Islington, on 8 January 2019. The cast, in alphabetical order, was as follows:

Dennis James Doherty
Maud Caroline Faber
Cynthia Alice Sykes

Director Alice Hamilton
Designer Delyth Evans
Lighting Designer Simon Gethin Jones
Sound Designer Ed Clarke

Characters

Cynthia
twenty

Maud
forty

Dennis
late forties

A forward slash (/) indicates an overlap in speech.

Act One

*Cynthia and Maud's living room. North London. This is
also where Cynthia sleeps. 6.30 a.m.*

Cynthia sits on the sofa, wide awake.

*She is dressed extravagantly, a cross between having
raided a fancy dress box and a child dressed up in her
mother's clothes: unsubtle make-up, costume jewellery,
feathers etc. Maud is slumped, fast asleep on the sofa.
She is dressed identically to Cynthia.*

*The room is dressed much the way Cynthia and Maud
have dressed themselves.*

*There is a clothes rack with clean washing neatly
hanging. A clock hangs on the wall. Cynthia has a
McDonald's chicken nugget meal in front of her. She
takes some candles out of a bag and carefully sticks them
into the chicken nuggets before lighting them.*

*She jumps up, blows a birthday hooter in Maud's ear
and begins to sing.*

Maud wakes with a start.

Cynthia
    Happy birthday to you
    happy birthday to you
    happy birthday dear Mouldy
    happy birthday to you.

Maud Christ.

Cynthia Happy birthday Moulds, look, candles.
    Blow them out, make a wish
    make three wishes if you want
    or ten or a hundred, or a thousand, or a million.
    You thought I forgot, didn't you?

9

But I didn't, course I didn't.
Go on, blow them out, blow them out.

Maud You what?

Cynthia Birthday candles, quick –

Half asleep, Maud attempts to blow out the candles.

Happy birthday to you
happy birthday to you
happy birthday dear Mouldy
happy birthday to you.

Maud is having no luck blowing them out.

Maud They're broke.

Cynthia squeals with laughter. Maud catches sight of the McDonald's bag.

McDonald's?
Where'd you get that from?

Cynthia Got you nuggets, Moulds, got you nuggets.
Six chicken nugget meal with Coke.
Large.

Maud You went out?
You went out to buy –
You left the house?

Cynthia Been planning this.

Maud And you went through with it?

Cynthia Blow them out!

Maud You actually really actually did? In real life?
This ain't some barmy dream is it?

Cynthia pinches Maud.

Ow. What d'you do that for?

Cynthia See, you're very much awake.

Maud Can't tell the difference sometimes.

Cynthia *The candles, Moulds.*

Maud is visibly buoyed by the news Cynthia has been to McDonald's. She tries, unsuccessfully, to blow the candles out again.

Maud Oh my Christ, I know what this is.
These are them bloody relightable candles, that's what they are.
Playing tricks on me, Cynth.

Cynthia squeals, hysterical with laughter.

Cynthia That's it. Playing tricks on you I am.

Maud That wax is making a right mess.

Cynthia Oh no. That's true what you've said there.
I'll blow them out.

Goes to blow them out, then visibly it dawns on her.

I forgot.
I'm a silly bloody sausage that's what I am.
I'll get some water.

Maud Don't want wax on the nuggets.

Cynthia We certainly don't.
You said a true thing there, we certainly don't.

Exit Cynthia.
Maud rifles around the sofa cushions and finds a packet of cigarettes.
She lights one using the candle.
Cynthia re-enters with a glass of water.

Shit, Moulds, wasn't quick enough.
Drips, little drips of wax on your nuggets.

She picks up each nugget and dips the end of the candle in the water.

Didn't think this through. Never even thought about the wax.

Little drips of wax.
It's not ruined, is it?

Maud takes a nugget and has a bite.

Maud Lovely. That's lovely that is.

Cynthia lets out a little squeal.
Maud alternates between her cigarette and her chicken nugget.

Thank you.
What a surprise.

Cynthia Six chicken nugget meal, *large*.
Do you wanna dance? I do. I wanna wiggle.

Maud I'm knackered.

Cynthia You've been fast asleep. Hours and hours and hours.

Cynthia types something into YouTube and presses 'play' on a video. It is the karaoke track to Shirley Bassey's 'The Greatest Performance of My Life'. She sings the first few lines, very over the top, serenading Maud who has begun to doze again on the sofa.

Wakey-wakey. You aren't even watching.
I've got a show for you.

She types something into the laptop, hands it to Maud.

Press 'play' when I say go.

Cynthia rushes behind the curtains, draws them across her body so that only her legs can be seen.

Go.

*Forced awake again, Maud presses 'play' on the
YouTube video. It is Shirley Bassey performing 'New
York, New York'.*

*As the song starts, Cynthia kicks her legs from
behind the curtains, her face still covered.*

*As the lyrics begin she bursts into the room,
contorting her face in an impression of Shirley Bassey.*

*Maud's phone beeps; she has received a text. She
looks at it and smiles before –*

Maud Shit.

Cynthia What?

Maud The alarm, the bloody alarm didn't go off.
Fucking phone, what's wrong with it?
Been sitting here eating chicken nuggets –

Cynthia I turned it off.

Maud You what? Why?

Cynthia It's your birthday –

Maud World don't stand still on my birthday. I've got
work.

She dashes out of the room.

Cynthia You didn't go last year.

*Maud rushes back in, wearing drab office attire. She
has wiped all the make-up off her face. She darts
around the room, looking for her stuff.*

Was that a text just now? Did you get a text? Who would
text you?
Are you really going?
What about my story?

Maud I'm late.

Cynthia How am I gonna sleep –

Exit Maud. We hear the front door slam.
    Cynthia contemplates for a second before flinging herself, frustrated, back on to the sofa.

SCENE TWO

Same day. 10 p.m.
    Cynthia has not changed her outfit since Maud left her this morning. She is still awake, sitting quite calmly.
    As Maud enters the living room, Cynthia springs into life.
    Maud is still wearing her work clothes but has brushed her hair and put some make-up on.

Cynthia You've been ages. Where you been?
    I was calling.

Maud sinks on to the sofa.

Maud Work.

Cynthia It's late.

Maud Worked late.

Cynthia You never work late.

Maud Did today.

Cynthia On your birthday?

Maud shrugs.

Then what?

Maud Then nothing.

Cynthia It's nearly ten o'clock.

Maud I'm going to bed.

Cynthia What? But it's still your birthday.

Maud I'll see you in the morning.

Cynthia I've been waiting all this time.

She flings herself at Maud on the sofa.

If I'm honest, Moulds, I've been moping about, waiting for you for far too long. And look at you, sitting there.
What's come over us? I for one can't stand it.
I suggest we buck up our ideas and buck them up fast.

Cynthia begins to move about restlessly.

What shall we do?
That sofa looks like it's eating you, Moulds. I can barely see you.
I'm gonna go to the bog one day, come and back and –

She screams.

'*Where's Moulds?*' I'll shriek.
She was here not two bloody bleeding minutes ago.
I know because I saw her.
We were having a natter and if I'm honest I didn't hear the front door go. Where would she have gone anyway?
Not shopping, not at this time of night.
Where's Moulds? I'll muse.
Well
muse is a bit mellow.
I'll be in a state of panic, you know I don't like being left on my own long. You know it panics me.
Then it'll hit me.
I'll see something out the corner of my beady little eye,
A waggling finger. And I'll say 'Hang on a minute.'
I'd recognise that waggling finger anywhere.
That there finger a-waggling belongs to my Moulds.
And you'll have been eaten by the sofa. Gobbled all up.
And then what will I do?
Eaten by the sofa and I'll be all by myself.
I won't know what to do, not if you've been eaten.

Are you listening? Please don't get eaten. Don't get gobbled.

Maud I'm going / to bed.

Cynthia Please don't get / gobbled.

Maud Why don't you try going to sleep?

Cynthia You're not going to sleep. Please stay awake with me.

Maud Got you these.

She takes some strawberry shoelaces out of her bag and tosses them towards Cynthia, who doesn't attempt to catch them. They land at her feet.
Maud, exhausted, leaves the room.

Cynthia We haven't even had dinner.

She picks up the sweets.

SCENE THREE

Next day. 6 a.m.
Cynthia has folded out the sofa bed and is sitting watching a video of Shirley Bassey's 'This is My Life' on the computer.
She is still awake. She is very, very tired.
Enter Maud in her pyjamas. She hands Cynthia a bowl of porridge.

Maud Sitting comfortable?

Cynthia gets comfortable and begins eating. During the course of the story she finishes her porridge and settles down to sleep.

The Story of Sylvie the Sooty Sparrow.
Once upon a time in a land far far away

somewhere near Manchester
up a tall tall tree there lived a little family of sparrows.
There was Mother Matilda, Father Fintan and their
four little babies,
Marcus
Richard
Jerry
and finally
Sylvie
whose feathers, unlike any other sparrow's, were a
sooty shade of grey. They were a very happy little family.
They did wholesome activities together
things like synchronised cheeping and leaf origami.
Saturday night, they watched telly on their four-inch
flat screen and no matter how much Father Fintan
pretended to snore through *X Factor*
they all knew he secretly had one eye open and a soft
spot for Cheryl. Now a long hot summer stretched ahead
and they had a holiday planned.
A resort in the Algarve particularly popular with all
them northern sparrows –

Cynthia Where's the Algarve?

Maud Portugal.
Mother Matilda had ordered four tiny little pairs of
flip-flops for the babies and as our story begins they were
trying them for size.
They were all lined up along the outside of the nest
prancing round and round in circles, showing off their
brand new footwear.
Red for Marcus
blue for Richard
orange for Jerry and of course
pink for Sylvie.
Suddenly, from nowhere a black cloud appeared
casting a dark shadow over the nest.

Thunder boomed and lightning forked.
The tiny baby sparrows wibble-wobbled round the edge of the nest. They flipped and flapped their weak wings
cheeping desperately for help.
Drops of rain the size of golf balls fell. Gale force winds howled.
This was climate change alright, two minutes ago it had been blooming forty degrees.
Disaster struck.
The four baby sparrows were flung from the nest.
Marcus, Richard and Jerry
killed, just like that.
And just as soon as the storm had started
poof. It was gone.
The sun returned to its scorching stool high in the sky
the clouds dissolved like sugar in tea
and the blue sky razzle-dazzled.
Mother Matilda and Father Fintan bombed out of the nest.
One by one they discovered the tiny little dead bodies of their tiny little babies.
First Marcus
then Richard
and finally Jerry.
Heartbroken, they hunted high and low for their only daughter
but Sylvie
dead or alive
weren't nowhere to be seen.
Finally, after hours and hours and hours of searching Matilda came across something that shattered what was left of her tiny sparrow heart.

Cynthia I don't like this story, it's sad.

Maud Underneath a great whopper of a dandelion she saw a little flash of hot pink.

Stomach sinking, she scooped up one tiny pink flip-flop.
The only trace of her daughter.
Presuming Sylvie had been gobbled by a hungry cat
with big sharp gnashers.
The grieving Matilda and Fintan fled
emigrating to Wales where they could at least bank
on rain
never wanting to be taken by surprise like that ever,
ever again.

*Maud opens her mouth to continue, sees Cynthia has
fallen fast asleep.*

*She shuts her eyes, takes a deep breath, and puts
her head in her hands. Remains like this for some
time.*

*As she looks up she notices what is on Cynthia's
laptop screen. It is a video of the two of them
performing to Shirley Bassey's 'This is My Life'.*

*Checking Cynthia is really asleep, Maud plays the
remainder of the film, smiles.*

*She gently pulls the duvet up over Cynthia, takes
the porridge bowl and leaves the room to get ready
for work.*

SCENE FOUR

Park. A Saturday afternoon.
Dennis and Maud are staring into a picnic hamper.

Dennis I panicked alright –

Maud Sure you didn't invite the whole office and I'm the
only one who turned up?

Dennis Trying to impress you, wasn't I?

Maud holds up the bottle of wine she has brought.

Maud Should have brought ten to wash down a 'ninety-eight piece party selection and twenty-four mini fresh fruit tartlets'.

Dennis These aren't just any mini fresh fruit tartlets.

Maud Oh yeah?

Dennis I mean, have a look
that ain't fucking Tesco.
I'll have you know Thierry dines exclusively from the M&S meat counter –

Maud Who –

Dennis My life partner.
Scotch egg?

Maud Your what?

Dennis My dog.

Maud *Oh.*

Dennis Go on then, what you got?
Goldfish? Micro pig? A harem of chinchillas?

Maud Just me.

He headers the Scotch egg he is holding towards Maud.

Dennis On your head –

Maud is taken by surprise. The Scotch egg bounces off her and falls to the floor.

Shit. Sorry.
Shit –
I didn't mean to attack you with a Scotch egg –

Maud I'll survive.

Dennis Reminds me of long car journeys.

Blackpool in the car
summer holiday, Mum and Dad screaming at each
other in the front
me in the back
two Scotch eggs
trumping all the way up the motorway.
Sorry that was
uncouth.

Maud Uncouth? Since when have you used words like uncouth?

Dennis Since I started going on dictionary.com.

Maud You what?

Dennis Lose the will to live in that hut, don't I?
My routine.
I read the newspaper cover to cover then sit on the internet bettering myself.

Maud Bettering yourself?

Dennis 'To better oneself.
To improve one's social standing, financial position, or education.'

Maud I know what it means.

Dennis Just get bored
all by myself.

Maud has begun to pour the wine into two plastic cups.

Not for me.

Maud No?

Dennis attempts to do kick-ups with the discarded Scotch egg.

Dennis International sports stars gotta watch it.

I'm not only an athlete
I am a brand.

Beat.

I'll have a little quiche though.

*He starts to take all of the food out of the hamper
and arrange it on the rug.*

Maud Very dainty.

Dennis 'Dainty.
Delicately small and pretty.
Dainty. Fastidious, especially concerning food.
A dainty appetite.'
Can I interest Madam in a tiny little sausage?
Dainty.

Maud I mean –

Dennis Shit. Was that –

Maud Uncouth?

They laugh.

Dennis I like your lipstick.
Very elegant.

Maud Blimey
Dennis from Security, what a charmer.

Dennis Sausage roll?

Maud Stop offering me sausages.

Dennis Oh Christ –

Maud I'm only joking.
Thanks for this, it's
lovely.

Dennis You sure?

I mean, I don't really –
I haven't really –
I don't go on
dates.

Maud Is this a date?

Dennis Oh. Well
maybe
I dunno.
What do you –
Why do you keep looking at your watch?

Maud Sorry, I didn't –

She pours herself some more wine.

Dennis You wanna leave, don't you?

Maud No –

Dennis You can if you want, I'm not keeping you here.
I wouldn't –
I mean, if –

Maud I don't wanna leave.

Dennis Sure?

Maud Sure.

Dennis Okay, good, because this is a lot of meat we've
got to get through here.
MEATFEST.
Or
not.
When –
When was the last time you went on a date?

Maud I don't –

Dennis Your birthday, Neil was giving you the eye.
Bet he'd like to ask you out on a date.

Maud Neil?

Dennis Fat Neil. Looks like a giant baby.

Maud Oh God, he reeks.

Dennis Shat in his colossal nappy. I wear Lynx, you know.
  Africa.
  Pork pie?

Maud Are you divorced?

Dennis Is it that obvious?

Maud I just like to
  know things. You know where you are with facts don't you?

Dennis Did you know Ted Bundy once saved a child from drowning?

Maud You got any?

Dennis Yeah, loads, facts are kind of my thing. Not showing off but –

Maud No. Offspring.

Dennis laughs.

What? What's funny?

Dennis You say funny words too. I like it.

Maud Have you?

Dennis Yeah.

Maud Go on then.

Dennis Oh. A son.

Maud How old –

Dennis Twenty-eight. Last week actually.

Maud Do anything nice?

Dennis Nothing special.

Maud What's he called?

Dennis We're like teenagers in the park here, ain't we?

Maud Bit fucking nippy.

Dennis Did you know that the *Titanic*'s head baker downed loads of whisky before he went in and that saved his life?
Kept his body temperature up.

Maud In that case –

She pours herself another wine.

Dennis I can
keep you
warm.
If
if you want.

He moves towards her and puts his arm round her.
    They sit awkwardly like this for a moment, both facing forward.

Nice the other night, weren't it? Your birthday.
I had a
nice time.

Just as Dennis turns and leans in to kiss Maud in a moment of panic she leans forward and shoves a mini-sausage in her mouth.

Oh –

Maud No –

Dennis Um –

Maud I was just suddenly really, really hungry.

Dennis Okay.

Maud Overcome with hunger.
That was lovely.
Yum.

Shoves another sausage in her mouth. Chews animatedly.

Have one.

They sit chewing their sausages.
There is a moment of stillness before they both launch forward and begin to kiss frantically.
They stop.
Both sit facing forwards.

Dennis Did you –
Did you know that one kiss requires one hundred and forty-six muscles to co-ordinate
including thirty-four facial muscles
and a hundred and twelve postural muscles?

Maud Dennis –

Dennis Sorry.

Dennis eats a Scotch egg.
Maud takes his hand.

SCENE FIVE

Cynthia and Maud's living room. Late that night.
They are wearing their matching outfits, singing to the finale of Shirley Bassey's 'I Am What I Am' together, which is playing on a YouTube video.
As their performance finishes they both collapse on to the sofa.

Cynthia Shirley Bassey's a vegetarian, you know.
Maybe I'll try vegetarianism.
I like courgettes and peas.

Maud Vegetarians don't eat chicken nuggets.
Knackered me out that has.

Cynthia Not me.

Maud Like one of them hamsters on a wheel you are.

Beat.

Good the other day though, getting them nuggets.
Going to get them.
Tried not to make too much fuss at the time
you know
make a big deal.
Couldn't believe it. So proud of you.

Beat.

Haven't stopped thinking about it.
Walked in, 'Six chicken nugget meal. *Large.*'

She beams at Cynthia, who looks away.

Be good to get out, wouldn't it?
Us two together.
Should go for a walk.

Cynthia Don't like walking.

Maud We could go on one of them buses round London.
Open-top.

Cynthia is silent.

Or you could come shopping with me.

Cynthia I was thinking about that.

Maud Yeah?

Cynthia I was thinking –
Why don't you just do internet shopping?
You're not very modern, Moulds.

Maud Don't want the faff.

Cynthia But then you wouldn't have to go out all the time.
You've been shopping more and more recently and I'm starting to think it's getting on top of you.

Beat.

I see the big vans out the window.
I see them driving up and down, stopping, delivering.
All you have to do is click click click.
Save your arms and legs.
You're always saying you're tired.
Well
I've found the solution.
Click click click and you won't be.

Maud How long we been here now?

Cynthia There's Tesco, Asda, Morrisons.
Or the posh ones.
Sainsbury's, well that's medium.
Ocado, that's Waitrose.
I like Tesco best, 'every little helps'.
If I'm honest they're bang on with that.
Shall we go on the website? I had a go earlier.
Thinking of your arms and legs, Moulds.

Maud Almost four years.

Cynthia I'll show you the basket. I put all sorts in. It's like a game.
(*On the computer.*) Click click click.

Maud Cynthia.

Cynthia I'm shopping.

Maud I don't need you to shop.

Cynthia I want to choose.

Maud Then come with me.

Cynthia No.

Maud Went McDonald's, same thing.

Cynthia It's not.

Maud Told you, I've been so proud.
Come on, I'll get my coat.
We'll go now. Tesco Metro's open late.
Come and choose. You can have whatever you want.

Cynthia No.

Maud Where's my shoes?

Cynthia I'm staying here.

Maud Don't be silly. McDonald's, Tesco's. What's –

Cynthia I didn't go.

Maud What?

Cynthia I didn't go to McDonald's.

Maud What, so fast food's falling from the sky these days, is it?
Flown in by wood pigeons?
You're right I needn't go shopping.
And what about them joke candles?
Delivered by a baby goblin on tiny roller skates?

Silence.

Where d'you get it from then?

Silence.

I give up.

Maud goes to leave the room.

Cynthia Sometimes I stand on the toilet and stick my head out the bathroom window and sniff up all the fresh air.

Beat.

I just wanted to do a special thing.
    Get you real, proper chicken nuggets.
    Not icy ones from the freezer.

Beat.

Just wanted to do a nice thing.

Maud is silent.

I went on Gumtree.

Maud Gumtree?

Cynthia It's a website.

Maud I know it's a bloody website, we got the sofa off it.

Cynthia Did some clicking. Found an advert.
    This boy, Eddie, think he's about twelve
    says he'll do anything for money.
    That's his advert.
    'Will do anything for money. London.'
    So he bought me McDonald's and party stuff and I gave him twenty quid.

Beat.

From your purse.
    Sorry.

Maud He came in here?

Cynthia Posted it through the letterbox, one nugget at a time.

Maud One chip at a time?

Cynthia The box fitted.

Maud appears to be silently crumbling.

Moulds?

*Cynthia moves towards Maud, tries to hug her. It is
uncomfortable.*
Eventually Maud responds.

Cynthia Love you.
(*Still hugging.*) Shall I show you how to add stuff to
your online basket?

Maud stiffens.

I knew you'd see sense.
Knew you'd come round eventually –

Maud You might think you'd heard the last of Sylvie the
Sooty Sparrow.
That her story had ended.
But you'd be wrong.
As it turned out Sylvie hadn't in fact fallen to her death
but instead landed slap bang in the middle of a molehill.
The force of her fall meant Sylvie ended up flying deep
down underground, giving Mary the mole a right scare as
she landed
without warning
on her kitchen / table.

Cynthia / Moulds?

Maud Listen.

Cynthia What are you doing? It's not –

Maud Shh –

Cynthia, unnerved and confused, does what she's told.

All the drama had left Sylvie weak and shaken and over the next few weeks kind Mary the mole nursed Sylvie back to health until she was well enough to pop back out into the open.

Sylvie searched high and low for her family but no one had a clue where Matilda and Fintan had zoomed off to.

Sylvie also began to notice something.

Lots of the other sparrows were looking at her funny and she could sense whispering as soon as her wings were turned.

She looked down and realised, they were laughing at her sooty feathers. Lost and lonely, Sylvie burrowed back underground where she knew she would be safe with Mary the mole.

With her family around her she never even noticed her sooty feathers. But now

all alone in a world of bronzy browny sparrows

Sylvie never wanted to leave the shadow of the burrow.

Thing is

Mary was a very old mole

and one day

to Sylvie's great sadness

she woke up to discover that Mary had peacefully shuffled off in her sleep.

'What will I do in a world without Mary?' Sylvie asked herself

cos as a sparrow she weren't able to survive underground

by herself.

Flapping and full of fear, Sylvie knew what she had to do.

She had to leave the safety of their dark lair and plop herself back into the sparrow community if she wanted to survive

no matter how scary that seemed.

After giving Mary a beaky kiss

thanking her for everything
including the sunglasses she was borrowing,
Sylvie surfaced.
The sun glinted on her wing.
As she crept into sparrow city, all them around her
marvelled.
Sylvie looked down and slowly she finally realised why
she'd been given her name.
She wasn't as she'd always thought
Sylvie the Sooty Sparrow.
No, she had grown up to be Sylvie the Silver Sparrow
and she was very special indeed.
Maybe everything is going to be alright in the end
she thought to herself
and it was.

Cynthia (*at the laptop*) So we'll go on Tesco then yeah?

Maud Until one day,
just as her parents had feared all them many moons ago
Sylvie was captured and gobbled by killer cat
who crunched and clawed her
until she was a messy mass of blood and guts.
In the end
all that was left to prove she ever even existed
was a single
silver feather.

Beat.

The end.

Beat.

Gonna stick to supermarket shopping.
Good for me arms and legs.

Maud leaves the room. Cynthia has been silenced.

SCENE SIX

Dennis's living room. A Saturday. 6 p.m.
Maud, wearing an Arsenal shirt, is studying a little
framed photograph. It is a family photo of Dennis, his
ex-wife and their son when he was a toddler.
She has a bottle of wine on the go.
Enter Dennis, also wearing an Arsenal shirt.

Dennis I'll provide stripy socks next time.

Maud Complete the look.

Dennis Full-kit wanker.

Maud Who you calling a wanker?

Dennis No –
That's just what –
It's just a phrase –

Maud I'm joking –

Dennis Knew that, course I did, I was just
bluffing, you know me.
Playing tricks on you. What a joker.

Beat.

You make me
nervous.
In a
in a good way.

Beat.

I'll tell you a secret.

Maud Go on.

Dennis Changed my mind.

34

Maud Oh come on, don't be a bore –

Dennis You can't
   laugh.
   Well
   what it is
   is.
   You ain't the only one
   other than me I mean –
   To have
   pranced around in that
   particular shirt –

Maud Excuse me?

Dennis Couple times, after a big win
      bit overexcited
      stuck it on Thierry
      give it a bit of that.

   Dennis mimes dancing with the dog.

Don't get Battersea on the blower, he loves it.
   Up on two feet.

   Dennis howls like an enthusiastic dog.

Maud Oh Christ. Make it stop.

Dennis You wear it better, my dear. Even if it is the dog's
   namesake.

Maud Namesake?

Dennis (*signals the back of the shirt*) Henry. Thierry
Henry.

Maud Who?

Dennis You're not even making a joke, are you, and
that's upsetting me.

Blasphemy, the full-kit wanker's never heard of Thierry Henry.

I ask you.

Maud goes back over to the photo she was looking at earlier.

Just so you know
    he's Arsenal's top scorer,
    he scored
    including during his loan from the New York Red Bulls in 2012 when he got four –

Maud This your –

Dennis Two hundred and fifty-eight league goals –

Maud This your wife?

Dennis Thirty-seven in both the 02–03 and 03–04 seasons –

Maud And son?

Dennis Leave that.

Maud Very cute.

Dennis Come here.

Dennis turns the photo face down.

Go on, you tell me a secret.
    Stop me blushing about the dog.

Maud Ain't got none.

Dennis Everyone's got secrets.

Maud shrugs.

I'd like to dance with you.

Maud I did line-dancing for a bit.

Dennis laughs.

Excuse me, least there weren't no dogs involved.

Dennis Line-dancing?

Maud I happen to like tassels.
Had a nice pair of boots. Looked the part.
Went on a Tuesday.
Stop laughing.

Dennis Sorry.

Maud Yeah well
there you go. That's my secret.

SCENE SEVEN

Same evening, 8 p.m. Cynthia and Maud's living room.
Cynthia is more extravagantly dressed up than ever.
The front door slams.
Maud enters, vaguely humming an Arsenal chant. She
is drunk.

Cynthia Where've you been?

Maud You're up.

Cynthia Where've you been?

Maud None of your business.

Cynthia It's Saturday.
You haven't been to work, so where?

Maud ignores her.

Why are you never here when I wake up any more?
Where do you go?

Maud takes a wine bottle out of a plastic bag she is
carrying and proceeds to swig it, still ignoring Cynthia.

37

I want to play. Why can't we play?

Cynthia applies some lipstick.

What are you wearing?
If I'm honest, you look very drab.
Where are your feathers? You need feathers.

Cynthia finds a feather boa and drapes it round Maud.

Bit of sparkle eh, Moulds? Sparkle and shine.
And as it goes, look at this glitter stuff I found.
You got it for me, remember?
Looks like deodorant doesn't it?
Roll on glitter.
Roll up and roll on, that's what I say, Moulds.

She brandishes the glitter stick.

Your face looks positively grey.
You've got the complexion of a rainy day.
Well, apart from your red-wine mouth.
Purple teeth.
Black tongue.
I saw it just now. Had a little peep.
Bit Illuminati, that.
You've been out boozing.
Keep waking up by myself, no one to talk to –

Maud Shut up.

Cynthia (*playfully*) No, you shut up.

Maud Please. I'm just not –

Cynthia Any fun any more? You got that right.

Maud I'm just
tired.

Cynthia I'm tired too.

Tired of waiting for you all night every night.
And you're never here. You're out there.
Or you're asleep
or you're –

Maud Please –

Cynthia I'm not doing anything.
I just want to dance. I wanna dance with Lance.
D'you remember him? Lance from *Neighbours*.
Was only a baby.
I used to say, 'I want to dance with Lance, I wanna
dance with Lance.' Over and over and over.
Toddling round on my fat little legs.
Will you be my Lance?
Shall we dance?
Lance?

Cynthia breaks into a frenzied cackle.
    Maud gets up and tries to leave the room.
    Cynthia darts in front of her, blocking the door.

Maud Move out of the way.

Cynthia Why?

Maud Get out of my way.

Cynthia You look awfully haggard.
I'm not being nasty –
You just
don't look like us.
Look, please, come and sit down.

She drags Maud over to the sofa.

I'll do your make-up.
You're just in time
just in time for *Britain's Got Talent*.
Do you want a drink? I'll make you a drink.
You've got your wine,
I'll get you a glass.

You can't drink out of the bottle.
How uncouth, that's awfully uncouth.
Thinking about it, Moulds, you're often quite uncouth.

Maud defiantly drinks from the wine bottle. Some wine trickles down her face.

You're just being silly now, acting like a silly little baby.
Look, I've got a glass for you.
There was a glass right here.
You're just being silent and silly, Moulds.
Silent and silly.
Give it to me and I'll pour it nicely.

Cynthia tries to grab the bottle, Maud clings on tight. They wrestle over the bottle until it slips from between them and lands on the floor.

Maud Look what you did.

Cynthia I was just trying to inject a tinge of decorum into our Saturday night.
I don't know what's wrong with you, I really don't.
It's only a bit of wine, now there's going to be a really nasty stain –

As Cynthia is speaking Maud lunges at her, pins her down and tries to cover her mouth for a moment of peace.

What / are you doing? Get off –
Get off me –

They struggle on the floor.

Maud Stop it. Just stop it.
I know what you're doing.
I know you can –
I see you
when you don't –
Sitting quietly, I –

Cynthia wrestles Maud away, pushing her off.
  Maud pushes her back, hard.
  Cynthia is stunned, they have never argued like this before.

Cynthia What the fuck are you doing?
  You've lost the plot –

Maud screams in frustration.

Where have you been?

Maud So you're my mum now, are you?

Cynthia Since when have you been mine?

Maud (*mimicking Cynthia*) 'I want to plaaay.'

Cynthia covers her ears and face.

There's a world outside that window
  you access it through the front door
  not the fucking letterbox.
  There's the sunshine as well, remember that?

Beat.

Out.
  I've been out.

A stunned silence. Maud has surprised herself.

I hate *Britain's Got Talent*.

Maud leaves the room.
  Cynthia stays as she is for a while. She desperately wants Maud to come back in.
  She doesn't.
  Cynthia turns on the television. The Britain's Got Talent *theme tune plays.*
  She is crying.

End of Act One.

Act Two

SCENE ONE

Weeks later. The middle of the night. Cynthia and Maud's living room.

The room appears neglected. Once shiny, now rusty.

There is no clean washing hanging on the rack; instead discarded clothes are strewn all over the place. There is dirty crockery littered around, including various porridge bowls. Alone in the house Cynthia performs Shirley Bassey's 'Secrets', along with a YouTube video; like karaoke but sad.

She potters around the room, plays with any remaining spoonfuls of porridge from a couple of the discarded bowls.

Settles back down to her laptop.

SCENE TWO

Dennis's living room. A Saturday evening.

Dennis and Maud are sitting on the sofa watching an Arsenal match, it is nearly finished. Maud is drinking wine.

Dennis COME ON, COME ON, NICE LITTLE FLICK.

Arsenal miss a good chance.

I tell you, moments like that, I wanna nut them all individually.

Bang their heads together until they bleed.

Beat.

Britain's Got Talent in a bit.

What d'you think? Simon Cowell and a curry?

42

Maud Lovely.

They continue to watch in silence for a minute.
Maud looks at Dennis. He is focused on the match.
She sips her wine and moves closer to him.
At this moment an Arsenal player is fouled.
Dennis lunges forward towards the screen.

Dennis No, ref, you fucking arsehole.
You fucking joking, you fucking titwank?
Don't look at him, you were right there two fucking feet away.
Red fucking card.
(*To Maud.*) You see that?

She nods.

(*To the telly.*) That's what I thought, wanker.
Look at him limping off on his little trotters.
Yeah yeah, mate, I'll ensure fucking BAFTA's aware of this little performance.
Dickhead.

Dennis sits back.
Maud puts a hand on his leg.
Dennis takes her hand and grips it.

Yeah, nerve-racking innit?
Don't worry, I reckon we'll make it.
Just.
They're down to ten men now anyway
could get lucky
rip a hole in their defence with the extra man
then we'd be sorted.

Maud shifts closer to him.

Oh come on, boys. HOLD UP PLAY.
What's the point if there's no one in the bloody box?

Dennis has let go of Maud's hand.

43

Her hand begins to wander towards his crotch.
He is so engrossed in the game that he doesn't notice.

Yes keeper. Boot it –

Suddenly he realises. Dennis looks down at Maud's hand on his crotch.
Slightly alarmed he turns to face her; they look at each other for a moment before they lunge.
They grapple around on the sofa.
Dennis is thoroughly torn between wanting to have sex with Maud and really wanting to watch the football. We can see this.
Quite quickly they begin to have sex.
Dennis can see the television over Maud's shoulder. He is obviously just about to come when –

GOOOAAAAALLLL.

Arsenal have scored in the final seconds of the match.
The whistle blows.
Dennis comes.
He looks down at Maud, mortified.

It wasn't because –
    I mean –
    That –
    Wasn't because –
    They weren't linked.

Maud is laughing.

I mean I can assure you of that.
    I don't want you to think –
    I mean, do you?
    You don't, do you?
    Oh Christ, you do.

Maud is laughing uncontrollably.

44

Dennis doesn't quite know how to react.
He begins to laugh. They are both in hysterics.
Eventually they collect themselves.
Dennis turns the telly off.

Just so you know –
   It wasn't –
   Just to be clear.
   It was you.
   Very nice.

Beat.

Important win though.

Maud Charming as ever.

Dennis Do you want some, um, tissue?

Maud Go on then.

Dennis leaves the room.
We can hear him speaking soppily to his dog in the background.
Maud arranges herself in the most dignified position she can and reaches for her wine. She looks pleased.
Dennis re-enters with a handful of loo roll, which he hands to Maud.

Don't look.

Dennis Sorry –

Dennis hastily spins round and stares intently at one patch of wall.

Maud I'm just gonna –

Dennis Yeah, yeah.

Maud leaves the room.
Dennis does a little celebratory dance.

He hears Maud on her way back. Composes himself, sits 'casually' on the sofa.
    Maud re-enters. She sits next to him.
    They look at each other, not quite sure what to say. He puts his arm round her.

That was nice.

Maud Bit quick.

Dennis looks mortified.

I'm joking.

Beat.

Was though.
    I'm joking, I promise I'm joking.

Dennis You on the, er –

Maud takes out her make-up bag and begins to faff with her appearance.

Because I mean –

Maud Don't worry about it.

Dennis I don't want to be a
    a killjoy or a
    mood-ruiner or nothing but I mean
    should
    probably pop down the pharmacy
    you know
    just in case –

Maud We're not about to have a baby, Dennis.

Dennis Well you never know, sometimes these things –

Maud I'm forty.

Dennis Jean just had twins at forty-six.

Maud Jean's a fucking miracle of modern science.
So is her hair.
I dunno how she gets –

Dennis I can't have a baby.

Maud We're not having a fucking baby.

Dennis Will you just –

Maud It's fine.

Dennis For my mind.

Maud I don't need –

Dennis Please.

Maud I can't
I can't, alright.
Have –
So just.
Okay.

Silence.
    Dennis's dog barks behind the closed door.

Your son.

Dennis says nothing.

Why don't you see him?

Dennis says nothing.

When was the last time?

Dennis Leave it, alright?

He reaches for the zapper and turns on the telly.
    The Britain's Got Talent *theme tune plays.*
    They stare at the screen in silence.
    Dennis turns the telly off.

I wanna say something.

Maud You don't –

Dennis How I been feeling recently –
Every time I see you –
Even on the security cameras, waiting for the lift –
Get this thing.
Feel happy.
Sounds creepy that.
I wanna
tell you stuff.
Try and remember stuff I've read in the newspaper
keep it in my head all day.
Sometimes I try so hard to remember I forget.
Before
when it was just –
It would all just stay in my head
I could remember
I could just say it
all that stuff I looked up
just –
You know.
But
now.
Started ripping stuff out
printing it off.
Pockets full of paper.

Beat.

Did you know there are over three hundred and sixty-five
different species of squirrels?

Maud I did not know that.

Dennis The red squirrel could be extinct in as little as
two decades.
The red squirrel and the hedgehog
they're under threat despite best efforts to protect them.
Gotta watch their backs.

He turns the television back on.

48

A couple of weeks later. Cynthia and Maud's living room. Evening.
  Cynthia is alone.
  She is sitting facing the computer, miming to a video of Shirley Bassey singing 'Without You'.
  She whistles to the instrumental at the end of the song, still staring intently at the screen. She stops the video; doesn't quite seem to know what to do with herself.
  She goes over to the window and peeps through a crack in the curtains.
  Looks at the clock.
  Lights a cigarette. Coughs.
  Thinks. Types something.

Cynthia The Algarve is the southernmost region of mainland Portugal.
  It has an area of five thousand four hundred and twelve square kilometres
  two thousand and ninety square miles
  with approximately four hundred and fifty-one thousand and five permanent inhabitants.
  In total
  including national visitors
  almost ten million people visit the Algarve annually.

  Beat.

Almost ten million people visit the Algarve annually.

  Cynthia leans forward and has another look at the screen, taking in what she has just read. She shuts her eyes and begins to recite.

The Algarve is the southernmost region of mainland Portugal.

49

It has an area of five thousand four hundred and
twelve square kilometres –

*She screws up her face trying to remember the next
bit. Exasperated she gives up, opens her eyes.*

Two thousand and ninety, two thousand and ninety.
Five thousand four hundred and twelve square
kilometres.
Two thousand and ninety square miles.
Okay.

Shuts her eyes again.

The Algarve is the southernmost region of mainland
Portugal.
It has an area of five thousand four hundred and
twelve square kilometres –

*We hear the front door slam. Cynthia leaps up. Maud
enters.*

Maud I'm off out.

Cynthia You just walked in.

Maud Got you a pizza.
Stick it in the freezer if you don't want it now.
You alright?
Right, I'll see you later.

Maud leaves.
  *Cynthia looks as if she is about to cry. Doesn't
allow herself to.*
  She takes out her phone and makes a call.
  It rings for ages until –

Cynthia Mum? Mum?
No it's me –
It's Alice.
Yeah –

Can you listen to me please?
Can't you –
No, no it's okay.
Just to
say hello.
Okay.
Bye.

She hurls her phone on to the sofa.
She begins to apply a lot more make-up.

SCENE FOUR

Dennis's living room.
Dennis and Maud are practising waltzing. Classical music plays from a YouTube video.
Dennis accidently treads on Maud's foot.

Maud Ow.

Dennis Shit.

Maud It's okay.

They continue to dance. Dennis treads on Maud's foot again.

Maud Ow.

Dennis Can't bloody do it, can I?

Maud Yeah you can.
Slowly like they taught us.
One, two, three. One, two, three.

Dennis Feet get in a fucking muddle.

Maud Really slow.
One, two, three.
Yeah that's it.

One, two, three. One, two, three.

Behind the closed door, Dennis's dog begins to bark.
Dennis is obviously trying really hard.

One, two, three. One, two, three. One, two, three.

Dennis Thierry. Put a sock in it.
Pain-in-the-arse wants to come in here.

Maud One, two, three. One, two, three.
One, two, three. One, two, three.

The dog's barking gets louder, more persistent.
As Dennis tries to concentrate on the steps he is
both distracted and wound up by the barking.
He tries to remain calm.

One, two, three. One, two, three.
One, two, three. One, two, three.

Dennis stands on Maud's foot. She grimaces, says
nothing.
The dog continues to bark.

One, two, three. One, two, three.
One, two –

Dennis steps the wrong way, attempts to move his
foot back into position quickly, twists his ankle. He
roars, half with pain, half frustration.
He storms over to the door, flinging it open, outside
the door. Thierry is thrilled to have finally been
acknowledged, jumps up at Dennis –

Dennis SHUT UP. I SAID SHUT UP.

He forcefully pushes Thierry away. The dog bounds
back up, thinking Dennis is playing.

GET. I SAID GET.

We hear a thud and a whimper.

Dennis has kicked him.

Go on. Get.

> *We hear him running away.*
> *Dennis comes back into the room. Slams door.*
> *Turns off the music.*
> *Maud is taken aback, wary.*
> *Dennis does not look at her.*
> *Silence.*

Sorry.

> *Silence.*

I'm really sorry.
  I just –
  I didn't mean –

> *Beat.*

Don't look at me like that.
  I'm sorry.
  Barking, was just the barking.
  And I'm a crap dancer.
  Always have been, dunno why we thought it was a good idea.
  Kept treading on your toes, didn't I?
  Sorry about that.
  You'll have swollen tootsies, my clown-feet stomping all over you.

Maud I'm gonna go. Tired.

Dennis Don't.

Maud I'm just really tired.

> *Desperate, Dennis runs and stands in front of the door, blocking Maud's exit.*

Dennis Stay, just for a bit.

I'm so sorry.

They look at each other.
  He moves out of the way.
  Maud leaves.
  Dennis stands stationary for a moment before he
kicks something.

Shit.

He feels sick.

SCENE FIVE

Cynthia and Maud's living room. 6 a.m.
  Cynthia is asleep in Maud's lap, clinging on to her.

Maud Once upon a time there was a couple of princesses.
  Unconnected.
  Couple of decades, couple of worlds apart.
  Princess Cynth and Princess Moulds.
  Very happy in their kingdoms.
  Cynth, the royal baby to a doting king and queen
  and Moulds
  betrothed to a lord.
  Two worlds floating about in their bubbles.
  Happy couldn't last. Bubbles burst.

  Beat.

King dies.
  Leaves his Queen and little Princess Cynth all alone.
  Queen's not one of them yummy mummies no more.
  Retired.
  Now she just sits inside
  sipping from her goblet all day
  all night.
  No banquets any more. Crisps for dinner.

Princess sleeping on the sofa because she's wet the bed.
Then on the floor because she's wet the sofa.
At her age.
The arguments begin.
Don't end until Princess Cynth packs her bag
don't come back from school one day.
Comes back, it starts again.
Same thing over and over until one day she don't come back.

Beat.

Princess Moulds on the other hand.
Royal wedding followed by a royal beating.
For a royally long time.
Till one day she run away too.
Hid away. Refuge.
Secret location, safe and sound.
Sort of.
Got herself together.
Million miles away from Monster.
That's his name now, she's never going back.
That's when they met in the middle.
Moulds kept coming across this twiglet.
Hard-nut had something about her.
See her all the time.
Sitting.
White Nikes in the gutter.
Bus stop
always about.
Needed someone.
Cut a long story short
brought her in.
Cynth and Moulds
new family.
Birthday.
Made a dressing-up box. Done lipstick.

First time Moulds had done lipstick since, before.
Like that but more.
Louder.
Redder.
Put on a show.
Wiggling and singing
prancing about.
Laughing and cheering
pulling on their beads and
they felt
safe.
Cynthia's birthday, chicken nuggets for tea.
Singing 'Happy Birthday'.
Real special occasion.

Beat.

New lives. All glitter and sparkles.
Two ladies in residence.
Once a month, beginning at least
Mummy's on the blower –
'Ring ring',
'Gobble gobble'
them two like fat turkeys for twenty minutes
just to reassure herself the runaway princess ain't dead.
But
all they need is their songs and their stories.
None of that other stuff
all grotty and infected worming its way in.
Happy ever after.

*Maud tries to stand up. In her sleep Cynthia clings
on, tight.*

   *Maud tries to prise her off, Cynthia continues to
cling on.*

   Maud gives up. Remains on the sofa.

That evening. Dennis's living room, the door to the hallway is open.
   He is leaving a message on Maud's answerphone.

Dennis Hello. Again.
   I'm sorry I keep –
   I just
   I don't mean to but suddenly I'm –
   I mean and then it's ringing and
   I just think that
   maybe this time you'll –
   Because
   all I wanna do is say sorry
   properly.
   I just want
   I just want you to –
   I just wanna
   hear your voice and –
   I mean I know I've left –
   I've
   seen you've been
   online.
   I know that sounds –
   But I don't –
   Earlier I just –
   It said last seen two minutes ago so I jut sat there
staring and –
   And then it said online again
   that was weird, because it's –
   I know what you're doing
   in that moment, you know?
   And I'm just there
   my belly all –
   And then you're gone again

57

and I sit waiting again
few minutes later you're back
and it's the same thing
keeps happening all day
and I just wanna know who you're talking to and
what you're saying and why isn't it me
then you're gone again and –
But you haven't blocked me so –

Beat.

Wanted to catch you after work
today I mean but –
You weren't –
Didn't see you arrive or –
Jean's back.
Looks knackered, even shows up on the cameras.
Thought about going down on my own but –
Well, you're my partner.
Been practising.
One, two, three. One, two, three –
Doing it in my living room, looking in the mirror.
Fucking perfect. Been practising every day.

He mimes waltzing with an imaginary partner.

One, two, three. One, two, three.
One, two, three. One, two, three.
One, two, three. One, two, three.
One, two, three. One, two, three.
So yeah.
I'm sorry. I'm so sorry.
I just wanna show you that I am.
Just wanna show you my dancing.
I've been practising.
Just wanna
I need to show you that I can do it right now.
I won't fuck it up.
Can you just –

Please.
Okay, well
bye then.
Bye.
Bye.
Give us a –
Please call me –
Okay.
Okay, bye.
Bye.

Dennis hangs up. He sits on the sofa.

Fuck sake.

He looks at his phone. Looks at the dog blanket on the cushion next to him.

Thierry. Thierry. Come in here.
Come on, boy.
Come on, come on.
Thierry.
Thierry.
Come and sit on the sofa with me.
Come on, come in here.
Come on, boy.
Please.

He opens a bag of treats.

Come on, look what I've got for you.
I'm sorry.
I'll just –
I'll leave this here for you.
I'll wait
I'll wait on the sofa.
Good boy.
You a good boy?
I'll just
sit here.

Same evening.

Cynthia and Maud's living room. 'Goldfinger' by Shirley Bassey plays on YouTube.

Cynthia performs the entire song, very much to Maud. There is something aggressive about it. The harder she tries to get her attention, the more she loses her.

She replaces the word 'gold' with 'mould'.

As Cynthia performs, Maud sits on the sofa.

Her phone rings. She watches it.

She gets a message.

She calls voicemail, listens.

Sits.

Her phone rings again.

She gets another text.

She calls her voicemail, listens.

Her phone rings again.

She sends a text.

As the song draws to a close Maud stands up.

Cynthia Where are you going?

Maud gets a text.

Who's that?

Maud hunts around the room for her shoes. She can't find them.

Maud Where's my shoes?
Where the fuck are my shoes?

Maud finds one shoe, puts it on.
Cynthia can see the other one.
She watches Maud looking.
Maud is getting worked up.
Maud's phone starts ringing, again.

Cynthia You gonna answer that?

Beat.

Dennis is gonna think you're dead.

Maud freezes. Stares at Cynthia.
Cynthia picks up Maud's shoe and hands it to her.

Maud Thank you.

SCENE EIGHT

The park. Dennis holds out a Tesco bag with loads of
different ready-made sandwiches in it.

Dennis I kind of
panicked.

Maud You didn't –

Dennis I know, I just –

Maud I'm not –

Dennis I didn't know which type to get
so –
I went in Tesco Metro.

Maud This isn't –

Dennis No I know, I just thought that
well
everyone likes a sandwich.

Maud I don't –

Dennis Please.

Maud still doesn't take the bag.

Thanks for –
I didn't think –

I'm sorry. I'm so sorry.
You look nice. Is that different make-up?

Beat.

Do you wanna –
    Can I show you –

Maud What?

Dennis My dancing.

Maud Not now.

Dennis No go on.
    Please.

Maud I said –

Dennis No, look look look.
    One, two, three.
    One, two, three.

Maud Stop.

Dennis One, two, three.
    One, two, three.

Maud Dennis.

Dennis Do you wanna –
    Look, I could get Mozart up on my phone –

Maud Dennis –

Dennis And then we could have a sandwich.

Maud I don't want a fucking sandwich.

Silence.

How's Thierry?

Dennis Yeah yeah, told you, he's fine.
    He's great.
    Good as gold.

Maud Should have brought him with.

Maud gets out a bottle of wine and two plastic cups.

Do you want a drink?

Dennis Don't drink, you know that.
I'm not only an athlete, I am a –

Maud Brand. I know.
But I'm having one so.
Then maybe you can show me your dancing.

She pours two glasses.
  Holds one out to Dennis.

Dennis I don't –

Maud Right.

Silence.

Dennis I don't know what to say.
I feel
speechless.

Maud You had a lot to say on them voicemails.

Dennis Sorry. Do you think I'm –
I felt. I just thought
I had it in my head
every time
the next time would be the time you'd pick up and –

Maud What would you have said?

Dennis Sorry. Sorry that I scared you.

Maud You think I was scared?

Dennis No.

Maud You just said you'd have said you were sorry that
you scared me.
Did you think I was scared?

Dennis I dunno.
  Yeah.

Maud What makes you think I was scared?

Dennis You looked
  scared.
  You left.

Maud Are you used to people feeling scared of you?

Dennis No.

Maud Has a
  woman ever
  been scared of you?

Dennis No.

Maud Just your dog?

Dennis Yeah. No, he's fine.
  NO.
  He's –

Maud Is he fine?

Dennis Yeah.

Maud Is it fine to kick your dog?

Dennis No.

Maud But he's fine?

Dennis Yeah, he's fine.

Maud That ever happened before?

Dennis No.

Maud Is he used to that?

Dennis No.

Maud Are you used to –

Dennis NO.

Maud What?

Dennis What?

Maud No what?
What was I gonna say?

Dennis I don't –
I don't know.

Maud You alright?

Dennis Yeah.

Maud You sure?

Dennis Yes.
I'm fine.

Maud Why don't you drink, Dennis?

Silence.
Maud has a sip of her wine.

That's lovely that.
The Californian grape.

Beat.

You know what, maybe we should just leave it.
This was a mistake.
Neither of us knows what to say.
I don't know why I –
I wasn't –
I'll just –

Dennis No, stay, please stay. I told you I'm
speechless.

Maud Why?

Dennis I don't know what to say.

Maud I just asked you a question. Answer my question.

Beat.

Why don't you drink, Dennis?

Silence.

Should I be worried?

Dennis No.

Maud You sure?

Dennis Stop it.
Please.

Maud What am I doing?

Dennis I don't know.

Maud What do you want?

Dennis I want –

Maud What?

Dennis For it to go back to
what it was like
before.

Beat.

Anytime I
care about
anything it gets
ruined.
Whenever I care about
someone
they
they make me
like –

Maud Like what?

Dennis Like
that.

Maud They *make* you –

Dennis I just
    I try really hard and it always get fucked
    and I get
    frustrated.

    Beat.

Someone told me I was charismatic once.
    Always remembered that.
    'Exercising a compelling charm which inspires
devotion in others.'
    Used to be a right diamond geez down the pub
    all the boys sat round listening to what I gotta say.
    King of that manor.
    Used to bring the little'un down. Next in line.
    He liked
    salt and vinegar crisps. Used to lick them and make
this kind of
    scrunched-up face. We'd all laugh and he'd do it again.
    Like a
    performance.
    Double act.

    Beat.

I was charismatic and we were
    happy.
    Three of us
    in our little
    castle.

    Beat.

Lost the
    charisma somewhere and
    s'pose all that was left was the
    pub.

    Beat.

Don't seem real no more. Any of that.
  Long time ago.

Maud Where are they now?

  Silence.

You've got no –

Dennis Come back from work one day –

  He shrugs.

Maud Were they scared of you?

Dennis No.

Maud I said were they scared of you?

  Silence.

Dennis Yeah.

Maud I was scared.

Dennis I'm sorry.
  I don't want –
  It's when
  it's when I care too much.
  I care so much I dunno what to do.
  When I –
  It's like I'm not there
  the real me and I –
  It's little things
  just little things and I get –
  And then I come back and I can see again and it's all
fucked.
  I wanna fix it, I wanna glue it back together
  but every time I try it's a bit more fucked.

  Beat.

But how it feels
  it's like no one cares as much as me.

68

Sometimes
    before
    when I got –

Maud Frustrated.

Dennis You just want some kind of response
    and
    and when you don't get one
    it's worse because it's like they don't care.
    Why don't they care?
    Why does no one care?
    And then they fuck off and leave you
    and it's just you and your mind and the phone and
    and then
    that's when you get a dog.
    But I'm not –
    That's why I don't –

    Indicates the wine.

I wanna be better, I wanna make myself better.
    I am better.
    I am better.

    Beat.

I wasn't
    expecting
    any of this.
    I wasn't
    prepared.
    I never thought –
    But you're all new.
    You're perfect and we watch football and we go
dancing.

    Maud shakes her head.

We do we do we do.

Dennis grabs Maud, tries to dance with her.

Look – one, two, three
  one two three.

He's dragging her about, it's not violent but it's uncomfortable.

Stand up, fucking stand up. Please.
  Please try properly. Look I'm really fucking trying.

He stops.

Sorry.
  I don't know what to do.

Maud I'm tired. I'm
  really
  really
  tired.

Dennis Me too.

Maud I just want –

Dennis What?

Maud I don't know.

Dennis You do.

Maud I don't.

Silence.

What do you want?

Dennis I told you, I wanna go back –

Maud No but, I mean
  what is it that you
  want?

Dennis I dunno. I dunno what you mean.

Maud If there was one thing that was –
You know?

Silence.

Dennis I want.
I want –
I want –

Dennis stops and shakes his head.
Maud shrugs, looks like she's going to leave.

I want
someone else to
believe that
I
to believe –
To believe that I can do something right.

Silence.

I told you I don't know what to say, I never know what
to say.
Sorry for –
Sorry for just –
Sorry I'm a shit dancer.

He turns to go.

Maud Don't.

Dennis What?

Maud I don't know. I want
I want you to stay.
I want to
tell you stuff.

Dennis I wanna tell you stuff too.
I wanna tell you everything.
I've got so much to tell you.

He reaches into his pockets, pulls out loads of little crumpled-up bits of paper.

Here we go, this is a good one.
    Did you know that about twenty per cent of meerkats are killed by other meerkats?

Maud I mean
    real stuff.
    Cynthia. /
    Her birthday coming up.

Dennis Who?

Maud Twenty-one.
    Was gonna have a little
    party.
    At our
    castle.

Dennis I don't –

Maud appraises the Tesco bag full of sandwiches.

Maud We prefer chicken nuggets.

Dennis You're not –

Maud No, I know. I'll
    get there.
    You know when I told you
    before
    well I never told you the whole –

Beat.

I gave up line-dancing because I was shit.

She holds out her hand to Dennis.

Do you wanna
    lead?

Act Three

A week later. Cynthia and Maud's living room. Evening.
The room has been decorated as if for a child's
birthday party.
They are both wearing new sparkles for the occasion.
They match again.
Cynthia carefully applies Maud's lipstick for her.

Cynthia Blood red. That's what this shade's called.

She finishes applying the lipstick.
Maud looks at herself in the mirror for a long time.

You sure we're having chicken nuggets? Promise?
Can't break tradition, Moulds, that would unnerve me
if I'm honest. Imagine if we had
I don't know
scampi
that would put me right on edge because it's not what
I associate with birthdays.
So I'm just making sure
because I've had a little look in the freezer and unless
you're hiding them from me somewhere to defrost
I can't see no nuggets and I'm getting a bit anxious.
So I'm just checking
just double-checking with you.

Maud There's nuggets. I promise.

Cynthia blows her hooter in celebration. She plays the
tune to 'Happy Birthday' on her hooter.

Cynthia Where is he then? I can't see him.
Moulds and Dennis sitting in a tree

K-I-S-S-I-N-G
First comes love, then comes marriage then comes a –

Maud Please.

Cynthia I'm only –

Maud Can you just –

Cynthia Why does he have to come anyway?
This is my birthday not an orgy.
Why do you keep looking at your watch?

Maud He's late.

Cynthia Maybe he's not coming. I don't think he's
coming.
In fact I know he's not coming.
He's on a mini-break to Copenhagen with his new
girlfriend, a younger model Moulds. He met her on
match.com.
She's twenty-six with a thong bikini and legs up to
here.
Her name is Ulrika.
Shall we
shall we just shut the curtains and watch the Berlin
concert?

Maud He'll be here.

Cynthia As you say, Moulds,
he's late.
Are infatuated men often tardy?
You've been dumped.
In swans Ulrika and we lose our Dennis forever.
I bet she's got great upper-body strength.

Maud receives a text.

Maud He says he's sorry he's running late. Thinks he's
nearly here.

Cynthia When he –
    When he's gone
    will you tell me the story of us again?
    Moulds –
    Moulds, will you?

Maud Yeah.

Cynthia Do you promise? Do you really promise?
    The story of Cynth and Moulds who both lived –

    Beat.

Who both lived –

Maud Happily ever after.

Cynthia Love you.

Maud Love you.

    They hug.

Cynthia All we need is us –

    *Plays the tune to The Beatles' 'All You Need is Love'
    on her hooter.*
        The doorbell rings. They look at each other.

Maud He's here.
    Ready?

    *Cynthia looks suddenly terrified. Rooted to the spot.
        The doorbell rings again.*

You ready?
    Cynthia.

    She shakes her head.

Maud I'll tell you the story of us.

    The doorbell rings again.

Come on, what are you? You're –

Cynthia Do you –
  Do you love me?

Maud Yes.

  Cynthia takes a deep breath.

Cynthia Ready.

  Maud goes to answer the front door.

I'll go.

  *She blows her party hooter before rushing out to
  answer the door.*
    We hear her open the door, she blows her hooter.
    Enter Dennis and Cynthia.
    *Dennis is wearing a suit and tie; he has slicked back
  his hair.*
    *He is holding a bunch of daffodils in one hand and
  a black bin-bag in the other.*
    Cynthia blows her hooter loudly in Dennis's ear.
  Dennis jumps.

Dennis Bloody hell.
  Alright?

  Dennis leans over to kiss Maud.
    Cynthia blows her hooter.

Jesus.

Cynthia Are you religious?

Dennis What? No?

Cynthia You said Jesus.

Dennis What?

Cynthia You said Jesus.
  I went – (*Blows her hooter.*)
  And you went Jesus. Are you religious?

Dennis Fancy dress is it?

76

Cynthia You look very Catholic to me. You've got Catholic hair.

Dennis Hope you like the flowers.

Maud They're –

Cynthia I like them.

Dennis Oh well, you can –
　　She can, can't she?
　　Mean, I brought them for you but –
　　Sorry, I –
　　Did I introduce myself?

He holds out his hand to Cynthia.

Dennis.

Cynthia That's an unusual name. Never met a Dennis.
　　Dennis the Menace, is that you all grown-up?
　　Tamed your hair and gone Catholic to repent for being such a menace?

Dennis is still holding his hand out. Cynthia spits on her hand and shakes his.

Where's Gnasher?

Dennis . . .

Cynthia Oh. Moulds, I made a faux pas.
　　Gnasher's dead.

Dennis Want me to put these in a vase? You got a vase?

Cynthia Gnasher's dead.

Dennis In the kitchen, or –

Cynthia Did he top himself?

Dennis What?

Cynthia Gnasher. Fling himself off a bridge on to a dual carriageway?

Dennis There ain't no –

Cynthia I realise that now. I was very insensitive.

Dennis I've got a dog.

Cynthia Had a dog.

Dennis Actually –

Cynthia I can barely understand what you're trying to get across, Menace.
  Just shut it for a minute, will you?

Dennis What?

Cynthia My name's Cynthia.

Dennis I know.

Cynthia And this is Moulds.

Dennis Moulds?

Cynthia We're very pleased to meet you.

Dennis Yeah, well,
  me and 'Moulds' –

Cynthia Moulds and I.

Dennis Moulds and I –

Cynthia I've heard all about you and Moulds. Like her a lot, I hear.

Dennis Yeah, yeah I do actually.

Cynthia That's a very intense thing to say. Are you an intense person?

Dennis I –

Cynthia Answer the question, I said do you like camping?

Dennis What?

Cynthia Where's your focus, Menace? I said are you an in-tents person?

I've got a four-man with a foyer. Do you like camping?
I love the great outdoors.
Ah, to be at one with Mother Nature.
DO YOU LIKE CAMPING?

Dennis I don't think I've ever –

Cynthia So your life's quite insular? Is that why you're so glass-eyed?

The deadening drill of routine.
There's a whole world out there, Menace.
Or is it cataracts?

She holds out both middle fingers.

How many fingers am I holding up?
(*Regarding the flowers.*) These are nice, did you choose?

Dennis Yeah –

Cynthia You telling porkies?

As it goes, you do resemble a giant suckling pig in a greasy wig.
Me and Moulds –

Dennis Moulds and I.

Cynthia Very good, Menace, that was a *test*.

But you musn't get cocky or we'll silence the suckling pig.
Sear you with my Bunsen burner and shove an apple in your gob.
The forbidden fruit.
I bet you know all about that from Bible studies.
Are you a door-knocker?
Is the end of the world nigh?
Do you live in the Watch Tower?

79

Dennis I live in Bruce Grove.

Cynthia I like flowers.
Not many flowers spring through carpet.
Not many flowers round this way.
I grow cress though.
I'll put them in water.

Exit Cynthia.

Dennis My God.

Maud You religious?

Dennis Don't you start, Jesus Christ.

Maud You sound religious?

Dennis I'm exhausted.

Maud I did warn –
You don't –
Shit, maybe this was –

Dennis No, she's –
She's, what's a good word?
Quirky?
I'm fine. Really. Looking forward to the soirée.

He embraces Maud.
Cynthia charges back into the room with a vase.

Cynthia Gimme those.

Dennis goes to pass Cynthia the flowers.
She rips them from his grip and begins to dismantle the neat bunch.
She tosses each daffodil into the water one by one.

A host of drowning daffodils.

Dennis Very artistic.

Cynthia blows her hooter in Dennis's face.

Cynthia When we having birthday nibbles?
Also
honestly what the hell is that you've got there?
Do you often drag bin-bags round with you? Is that
your man bag?
What's in there? Dead body? A corpse?
Shall we hack it to pieces and hide it in the walls?
You'd have to go and fetch the cement-mixer from
upstairs.
It's in the bathroom, doubles as a bidet.
No but really, I didn't realise you were a necrophiliac.
It's not that sort of party, Menace.
Why are you getting your phone out? That's poor
etiquette.
Texting Ulrika?

Dennis What?

Cynthia Who you texting?

Dennis No one. I'm looking up that word.
Necro what?

Cynthia Necrophilia? The act of shagging a dead corpse,
Menace. /
Fucking a cadaver, is that more poetic?

Dennis WHAT –

Cynthia Oh, don't look at me like that, it's only a joke.
It's only a joke, Menace. I'm a stand-up comedian.
I have hundreds of awards, you'll see them mounted in
the bog above the bidet.
Do you get the shits a lot?
DON'T ANSWER THAT.
Come on then, what's in the bag?

Maud What is in the bag?

Dennis Well

it's the reason I was late.
So, I went to McDonald's –

Cynthia *McDonald's?*
Moulds, did he just say McDonald's?

Dennis So I went up to the counter, right –

Cynthia rushes over to the bin-bag and tears it open.

Cynthia Thought you were playing tricks on me Moulds.
Empty freezer, empty of you know what at least –
Plenty of peas and sweetcorn.
But you promised, looked me in the eye and said
'I promise'.
Started thinking you were up to something.
Lo and behold, who comes creeping down the corridor
with his Catholic hair and unusual name?
That was a masterstroke if I ever saw one, you're so
clever.
You cheeky bloody monster.

Cynthia begins to unpack the bin-bag.

What's all this, Menace?

Dennis Chicken nuggets. Chips.

Cynthia Meals?

Dennis Yeah.

Cynthia What size?

Dennis Large.

Cynthia LARGE.

She continues to unpack the bin-bag.

Maud How many –

Dennis Yeah, so
that's what I was –
There was a long queue, a really long queue

kids everywhere
crawling about like
maggots
one of them did a fart on my foot.
Saturday innit. I queued for about twenty minutes.
I finally get to the front and I'm gonna say three six
chicken nugget meals, large
but
but I panicked, I hear myself
I just hear myself saying thirty and she goes thirty?
Like she'd heard wrong, made a mistake
and I just go
yeah thirty, I'm off to a party.
So then they're bringing out all these bags, looking at
me a bit weird and I think, shit
I've only got two hands, I've already got the flowers
so really I've only got one hand.
So I pay and again I think, shit
but then I had this idea
I was in the Tottenham branch so I only live down the
road
I got them to keep them there for me
I run home get a bin-bag, shift it all in –
I didn't know what to do with the Cokes
I left them –

Cynthia I need the caffeine.

Dennis But that's why I'm late.

Cynthia Unfashionably late.

Dennis Sorry.

Cynthia screams.

What?

Cynthia Moulds, you know what's only gone and
happened.

83

Maud What's gone and happened?

Cynthia I think you can guess –

Maud I think I might well be able to guess –

Dennis What's happened?

Cynthia Can't you guess?

Dennis No?

Maud You can't guess what's happened?

Dennis I can't guess what's happened.

Cynthia Are you even trying to work it out?

Maud Doesn't look very much like you're trying.

Cynthia Use your noggin, Menace.

Maud Have a think.

Dennis What d'you mean? Nothing's happened.

Cynthia Apart from the one thing that has.

Dennis I dunno, can you tell me?

Cynthia Can't just be told everything. Gotta use your brains.

Dennis I didn't see anything.

Cynthia No one *saw* anything.

Maud We didn't *see* it.

Dennis I give up.

Cynthia You give up?
   He gives up.

Maud He's given up.

Dennis I give up.

Cynthia Well, why didn't you just say you didn't know? Why didn't he just say?

Maud I dunno. You could've just said.

Dennis Said what?

Maud That you didn't know.

Dennis Didn't know what you were talking about.

Cynthia Didn't know what we were talking about?

Dennis No.

Cynthia Well, why didn't you say before?

Dennis I did –

Maud Did what? Did know? So why did you say you didn't?

Dennis I didn't say I didn't, I said I did –

Cynthia You can't be so cryptic, Menace.
If I'm honest neither me nor Moulds knows what the bloody hell you're going on about.
All I said was 'Oh look what's happened, cold chicken nuggets, should probably stick them in the microwave' and you went off on one.
Shouting and screaming at us.
Are you normally so irritable?
Is he normally so irritable?

Maud It's only a silly game.

Cynthia Yeah it's called FUCK UP A STRANGER.
Play it all the time.
It's only a joke, look at his face.
Don't look so alarmed, Menace, you are aware of my awards.

Dennis Misunderstood.
It was a misunderstanding.

Cynthia Do you have a lot of misunderstandings, Menace?

Do you find it quite hard to communicate with other people?

I've found in the short time we've known each other that you tend to mumble.

Do you have a speech impediment?

Dennis No.

Cynthia Are you nervous in front of women?

Dennis No.

Cynthia I'm just musing.

Next on my schedule is microwaving.

She scoops up the McDonald's and leaves for the kitchen.

Dennis What was all that? You were –

Maud Gotta play along, keep her sweet.

Dennis Taking the piss out of me –

Maud I wasn't.

Dennis You were.

Maud It's her birthday.

Dennis Sorry.

In the background the microwave pings.
Maud pours a very large glass of wine. She glugs it.
Dennis moves closer to her, affectionate.
Enter Cynthia; she blows her party hooter.
Dennis, startled, leaps away from Maud.

Cynthia Right, batch number one.

Piping hot. Hope you don't burn your tongue, Menace, couldn't have that. Imagine that, if you burnt your tongue.

Wouldn't be able to enjoy the rest of the party I imagine, so be careful with those nuggets.

Watch your tongue.

Cynthia is arranging candles in the chicken nuggets.
She lights them.

LET'S SING.
  Happy birthday to ME –

  Beat.

Oh come on, Menace, its my birthday. I've lit the bloody
candles.
  Gotta do everything round here, haven't I?
  As it goes, you're supposed to sing.
  You two gotta sing in harmony because that's birthday
tradition.
  Then I blow out the candles
  then we'll eat our nuggets and continue to have a
wonderful time.
  That's tradition, that's birthdays.
  Peace and harmony
  joy and happiness
  chicken and singing
  musical chairs
  that's birthdays.
  But you've gotta sing or its gonna be ruined and you
don't want that on your conscience.
  I know I wouldn't.

Maud Come on.

  Maud starts singing. Dennis quickly joins in. Cynthia
  conducts.

  Happy birthday to you –

Dennis
  Happy birthday to you
  happy birthday dear Cynthia

  At this point Cynthia interjects and sings 'ME'.

  Happy birthday to you.

For she's a jolly good fellow
for she's a jolly good fellow
for she's a jolly good fellow /
and so say all of us –

Cynthia That's the spirit, look, he's getting into it –
ADORE ME, DENNIS.

Dennis And so say all of us.
And so say all of us.
For she –

Cynthia gasps.

Cynthia THE CANDLES.
Look at that –
Little drips.
Little drips of wax drip-drip-dripping on the nuggets.
Shit.
Gotta blow them out.
Menace, YOU blow them out for me.

Dennis It's your birthday.

Cynthia So you must bow down to my demands.
I'll make a wish.

Dennis shrugs. He leans forward to blow out the candles.
    They stay lit.
    Cynthia squeals with laughter.
    Dennis tries again.

Dennis These some sort of joke?

Cynthia Playing tricks on you.
(*To Maud.*) You knew, didn't you?
Remembered. Remembered from last time.

Dennis tries to blow out the candles again. Cynthia squeals.

Dennis I give up.

Cynthia Seems to be a habit of yours.
In the short time we've known each other I've picked up on some character traits.
Catholic
poor communicator
giver-upper.
An attractive package to offer a lady.

Dennis Watch it, you.

Cynthia What am I watching?
Is *Gogglebox* on?
Those cataracts giving you gyp? Playing up are they?
Come on, let's eat.
Let the birthday feast *com-menace*.

She deposits the candles one by one into the vase of flowers.

So there's not much chit-chat going on, is there?
At parties people mingle. We've got to mingle with each other.
Been on any nice holidays recently, Menace?

Dennis No.

Cynthia Not camping, we've established that.
What about more broadly, not into holidaying?
You hate it, do you?

Dennis No, I like –

Cynthia Then why don't you? Let's unpack this.
No one to go with.

Dennis Something like –

Cynthia Most recently I found myself in the Algarve.
Moulds and I frequently jet-set.
We love to holiday.

Maud We do love holidaying.

Cynthia We absolutely love to holiday.

Dennis Never mentioned it.

Cynthia It was very recently actually.

Dennis Spain, innit?

Cynthia The Algarve is the southernmost region
of mainland Portugal.
   It has an area of five thousand four hundred and
twelve square kilometres
   two thousand and ninety square miles
   with approximately / four hundred and fifty-one
thousand and five permanent inhabitants –

Dennis Okay
   yep
   got the / idea.

Cynthia In total
   including national visitors
   almost ten million people visit the Algarve annually.
   Don't you know anything, Menace?
   How many people visit you annually?

Dennis Nowhere does chicken nuggets like McDonald's.

Cynthia I'll drink to that, Menace, I'll drink to that.
   To be fair, that's the first sensible thing you've said
since you stepped foot in here.
   Little gold nugget
   d'you get it?
   In amongst a shedload of shit spewing from your gob.

Dennis Fucking hell, princess –

Cynthia You got any more gold?
   Or are you just a boring fuck?

Maud Cynthia –

Dennis Look, have I done something –

Cynthia Boring Catholic fuck.

Maud Stop it.

Cynthia Stop what?

Maud She's just –

Dennis I don't understand –

Cynthia Catholicism is a broad term for describing specific traditions in the Christian churches
in theology and doctrine
   liturgy /
   ethics
   and spirituality –

Dennis stands up suddenly.

Dennis Need a piss –

Maud Top of the stairs.

Exit Dennis.
   Maud shuts the door.
   Cynthia begins to hyperventilate.

Cynthia I don't like it. I can't –

Maud You can, he's –

Cynthia I don't want him here. Make him leave, please make him leave.

Maud You don't have to –
   You could just be –
   Why don't you –

Cynthia I want
   I wanna go
   to –
   I can't breathe, I need –
   I want
   air.

Maud Do you wanna go outside?

Cynthia No.

Maud You're doing
     really well.
     He likes you.

Cynthia Please. I want –
     Can we go to John Lewis?
     I'll be sick –
     We can just go
     now
     and when he comes back we'll be gone, then he'll leave.

Maud I don't want –

Cynthia Can we go to John Lewis?
     Please?

Maud I don't want him to leave.

Cynthia Please can we go to John Lewis?

Maud We're not –

We hear Dennis coming down the stairs.
     Cynthia is still hyperventilating.
     Dennis enters.

Cynthia (*picking up as if she never left off*) For many the
term usually refers to Christians and churches –

Dennis Look, I know what a fucking Catholic is, alright?

Cynthia slams the door.

Cynthia Don't ask stupid questions then.
     Come on, we're mingling. Tell me all about yourself.
     What's the worst thing you've ever done?

Dennis turns to Maud.

Do not ignore a princess on her birthday.

Dennis Have I done something to upset you, sweetheart?

Cynthia Not in the slightest. Why would you think that?

Dennis I dunno –

Cynthia Have a drink, Menace. Chillax.

Maud He doesn't –

Dennis I don't drink.

Cynthia Oh surprise, surprise from the boring fuck.
No wonder you're so uptight.

Maud Don't take any notice –

Cynthia Who invited this boring fuck to my birthday?
I'm twenty-one today. I'm in my prime.
How old are you, Menace?
You look about sixty-five.
Am I right?
Do you live alone? Expect you'll die alone at this rate.

Maud You're not being very nice to poor old Dennis –

Dennis I'm not old –

Maud pours herself some wine.

Cynthia Some for me, plenty for me
and for –
Oh wait, no –

*Cynthia holds out a glass to Maud; she hesitates
before pouring her some.*

Maud Settle your nerves.

Cynthia My state is positively meditative.
Is that a tic you've got, Menace?

*Dennis snatches the bottle from Maud and pours
himself a large glass, which he downs. He pours
himself another.*

Finally you've got a grip and joined the party. Nice one,
Menace.

Dennis Cheers.

Cynthia What are we toasting? Are you another one of my new dads?

Maud Stop it.

Dennis shoots Maud a look.

Cynthia Why can no one take a fucking joke?
IT'S MY BIRTHDAY AND I'LL LIE IF I WANT TO.

Dennis To Cynthia, who is in her prime.

Maud Who is in her prime.

Cynthia Wait there. Don't move a muscle. I'll know.
You mark my words Menace, I've got a seventh sense.

Exit Cynthia.

Dennis What did she mean?

Maud Nothing. She said it herself.

Dennis Didn't sound like nothing.

He refills both of their glasses.

It's only a glass. I can have one glass.

Maud Are you –
Dennis, I dunno.
Maybe this –

Dennis What?

Maud Maybe –

Dennis I've seen the way other geezers look at you. I told you, Neil –

Maud No one wants that smell in their home.

Dennis He's been here? When?

Maud No, I was only joking. You're being silly.

Dennis I'm being serious –

Maud She's winding you up.
What did I say? What did I say she'd be like?
Remember?
Are you listening to me?

There is a crash from the kitchen.

Dennis Christ, what's she fucking doing now?

Maud I'll check –

Dennis (*grabs Maud by the arm*) Stay with me.
I like your lipstick.

Pulls her towards him, kisses her.
Enter Cynthia.
She stops in the doorway for a moment. Stares,
then bursts in.
Cynthia is holding a large jug full of a murky
brown liquid.

Cynthia Seeing as you've finally entered into the party
spirit, Menace,
I've made a *cocktail*.
Don't look at me like that.
If I'm completely honest, yes, it looks like I've shat
directly into this jug but I can assure you that's simply
not the case.
I learnt the recipe on our recent holiday.
I have also got *straws*.
Musical chairs. Let's play musical chairs.
Make it silly, like you, Menace.
Loser every round drinks.

Maud No.

Cynthia You got him round here for a party, Moulds,
not a wake.
Have I misunderstood the premise?
Drinking and dancing?

She slurps from the jug.

95

Maud You don't –

Cynthia You can talk. Have another wine.
Arrange the chairs, I'll sort out the music.
Menace, you buck up.

Dennis is eyeing the wine bottle.

Dennis There's only three of us. Who's gonna turn the music off?

Cynthia Very perceptive, Menace. Only two play at a time.

Dennis Two people round one chair?

Cynthia Are you having problems communicating again, Menace?

Dennis So it's just two people playing round one chair?

Cynthia I've explained the rules.

Maud I don't think –

Cynthia I'm master of the music, lord of the dance.
When I press 'play', you, my little minions, will dance around the chair of treachery.
When I press 'pause', you will lock horns and battle for its comfy cushion.
Whoever fails in their quest
Menace
will drink the Algarvian liquor and
master of the music, lord of the dance
me
will reset and we'll start again.
Understand, Moulds?

Maud Yes.

While no one is looking, Dennis takes a large swig of Maud's wine.

Understand, Menace?

Dennis So it's us two round this chair?

Cynthia PROCEED.

Cynthia presses 'play' on the laptop, Shirley Bassey's version of Pink's 'Let's Get the Party Started' plays.
Dennis and Maud dance round the chair.
Dennis is self-conscious. Maud begins to relax.

More wiggling, Menace.

They move round the chair for a while before Cynthia pauses the song.
Maud wins the chair easily.

Not trying hard enough, Menace.

Dennis It's Dennis.

Cynthia Drink.

He drinks.

You made a right suckling-pig-in-a-greasy-wig's ear of that.
Try harder this time. It isn't a game.
Back in your positions.

Cynthia presses 'play'.
They move around the chair again.
Cynthia pauses the music.
Dennis makes an effort to move quickly but Maud wins the chair.

Maud HA.

Dennis I'll get you.

Cynthia Menace.

Cynthia points towards the cocktail.

He's very elegant with a straw, isn't he?
Come on, loser, back in position.

She presses 'play'.

They begin to wiggle around the chair once more.
She leaves the music on for longer this time before
she pauses it.
Both Dennis and Maud scramble for the chair.
Maud just gets there before Dennis pushes her on
to the floor.
He barely notices, relishing his victory.

Dennis WHO'S THE FUCKING KING NOW?

Cynthia Look what you've done, Menace, you've killed
Moulds.
What's all this brattitude you're displaying? It's only
a game.

Dennis Shit.
Sorry.
Got caught up –
Let me help you –

Maud I'm fine.

Cynthia Passion and drive are what musical chairs
intends.

Dennis Bit wobbly –

Cynthia Wibble-wobble
wibble-wobble
Menace on a plate.

Dennis Too much lard on me.

Cynthia You're very fleshy.

Dennis Don't just sit there, take my hand.

Cynthia Are you okay, Moulds, after your near-death
experience?

Maud Fine.
Saturday night, shall we put the telly on?

Cynthia Wouldn't dream of it.

What's got into you, Moulds? You've hardly said anything the whole night and now you want to put on your slippers and watch *Take Me Out*.

IT IS MY BIRTHDAY.

THIS IS A PARTY.

She reaches for a balloon, bites a hole and inhales.
She sings 'Happy Birthday' to herself, pretending it was a helium balloon.

I'm bored. You bored, Menace?

Dennis No.

Cynthia Have you got the internet, Menace?

Dennis Yeah.

Dennis Yeah.

Cynthia There's lots of stuff on the internet.

Argos

eBay, that's good, best game on there.

I bought a car once and this other player started sending me sweary messages which was

unkind.

Actually, to be fair, it's overwhelmingly flawed.

The game itself is really fun

the rush of final seconds

the ticking clock

five

four

three

two

one

'Congratulations, you have won this item.'

But the other players are very irritable characters and can be quite hurtful.

Don't think they understand the rules.

Oh well, there's other stuff too.

Lots of rude ladies on the internet.

Maud Enough.

Cynthia We love YouTube.
Then there's Wikipedia. Dictionary.com.
I've got rectangle eyes.
What's your favourite thing on the internet?
Rude ladies, is it?

Maud Shut up.

Cynthia Love a bit of RedTube, lonely old man like you?

Maud Shut up.

Cynthia Channelling your pent-up lust all over your desktop.

Maud Shut up.

Cynthia Is your keyboard very congealed?

Maud I SAID –
Dennis, I think you –

Dennis I'm staying.

Maud No, I really –

Cynthia bounds over to him.

Cynthia I'm only joking. You know what I'm like. Bit of banter. Lads together.

Beat.

Can I put lipstick on you?

Dennis No fucking way.

Cynthia I thought you were a modern man.

Applies more lipstick herself.

Polyamory is very modern, Menace.

Dennis Poly-fucking-what?

Cynthia Not gonna look it up on your phone?

'The practice, state or ability of having more than one sexual loving relationship at the same time, with the full knowledge and consent of all partners involved.' /

One of my new dads, aren't you?

One of many.

You gonna tell me a bedtime story later? / Can't sleep otherwise –

Maud STOP IT. SHUT UP, THIS ISN'T A GAME ANY MORE. SHUT UP, SHUT UP, SHUT UP.

Dennis How many?

Cynthia You don't know?

Maud SHE'S LYING.

Cynthia Telling porkies, am I?

Dennis HOW MANY?

Dennis is standing over Cynthia.

Cynthia I don't count on my fingers.

I'm not that way inclined. I'll need my abacus.

Maud Dennis –

Cynthia You're a fucking idiot coming round here, it's not my birthday.

Not my birthday for months.

Get you round. Make you feel special.

What did she say about me? It varies.

Dennis turns to look at Maud and back at Cynthia.

This is what Mouldy dearest does.

We have a lot of parties.

No one's ever brought two hundred nuggets though, I'll give you that.

Dunno what she's told you but

put it this way

she does a lot of dancing, *negotiates* a lot of dick –

Dennis is about to lose it. Pre-empting the danger,
Maud panics.
   She picks up a bottle of wine and smashes it over
his head.
   Dennis falls to the ground.
   Silence.
   Maud is sick.
   Cynthia looks like she is about to try and say
something.

Maud Don't.

   Beat.

Just.
   Don't.

   Silence.
   Maud composes herself.
   She opens the bottle of wine, pours herself a glass.
Sips it.
   Cynthia doesn't move.

That's lovely. Paid the extra.
   Worth it, not just cheap plonk.

   Beat.

You two bores. What's wrong with you?
   It's early.
   Fine.
   I'll provide the entertainment.
   Got a story for you.
   That's what people do at parties, isn't it? When they're
mingling.
   Tell amusing anecdotes. Little ditties.
   Cynthia loves a story.
   Don't you?

   Cynthia remains silent.

Let's do
Menace the honour.
This is a good one.
Monsters, princesses locked away in castles –
Yeah, this one's got it all.
The story of us.
Songs and stories, glitter and sparkles
Cynth and Moulds.

Beat.

Then this bloke, nice bloke, only bloke I've ever felt
settled round since
before
asks me to come down the park with him.
Felt alright. Felt safe.
And he's telling me these facts, obsessed with facts.
He's talking about his dog and
going on and on and on and on and on about football.
And I'm
laughing again.
And I'm
secretly watching
Match of the Day.
Then
it all comes
crashing down. Because
bubble burst.
Again.
But that's life innit?
Things don't change no matter how much you want
them to.
You try, you run away
you make things new but they're not.
It's just
same old shit covered in lipstick.

Beat.

Unusual name, Cynthia. Don't you think, Menace?

Beat.

She's not real.

Cynthia's a silly voice and a dressing-up box.

Alice is real. But Alice ain't nothing really like Cynthia at all.

Alice pronounces all her 't's and excelled at GCSE.

Beat.

Lost a bit of its atmosphere, this party.

Its 'ambience'.

Let's put that right.

I've got a wonderful voice.

Downs wine from the bottle.

The karaoke track for Shirley Bassey's 'The Greatest Performance of My Life' plays.

Maud, word perfect, gives the performance of her life.

Then she walks over to Dennis, checks his pulse and whether he is breathing.

He is.

She picks up her mobile phone, dials 999.

We hear the phone ringing. An operator picks up.

Ambulance.

Maud places the phone down.

We can hear the operator asking for the address in the background, asking if Maud is still there etc.

Maud picks up her handbag, checks herself in the mirror and leaves the house.

Blackout.

End.